Head Over Heels

An Adult Coloring Book for Fashionistas and Shopaholics

* Test page at end of book

Published By
RW Squared Media

———————

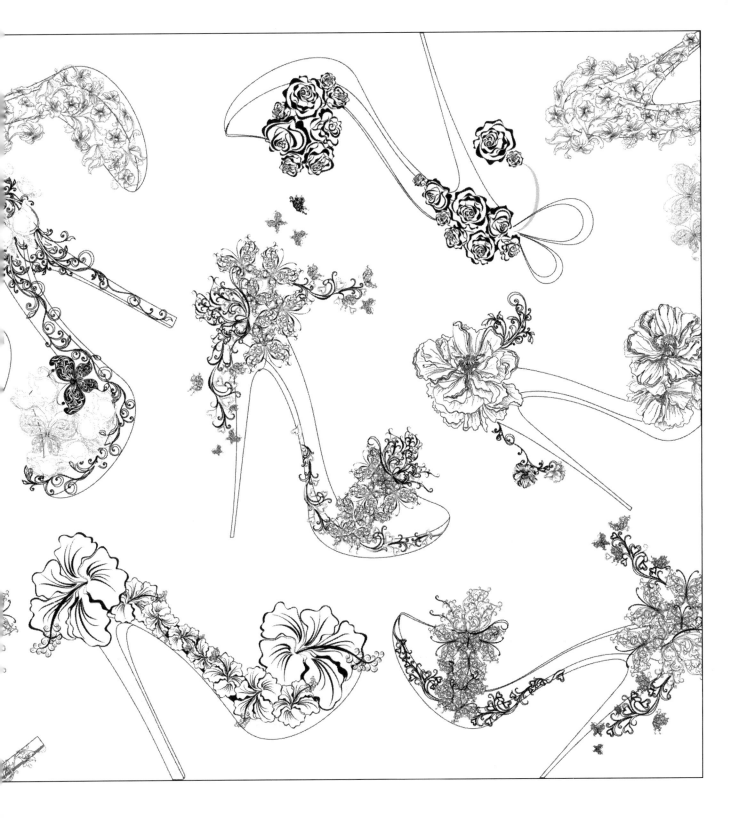

Other amazing adult coloring books available on Amazon.com:

*The Adult Coloring Book of
Amazing Faces and Abstract Art*

*Mandalas and More
Adult Coloring Book*

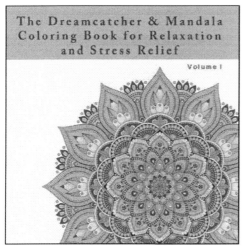

*The Dreamcatcher & Mandala
Coloring Book for Relaxation and
Stress Relief*

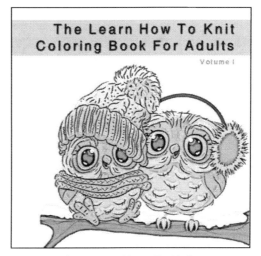

*The Learn How To Knit
Coloring Book for Adults*

RWSquaredMedia.Wordpress.com

Test Page

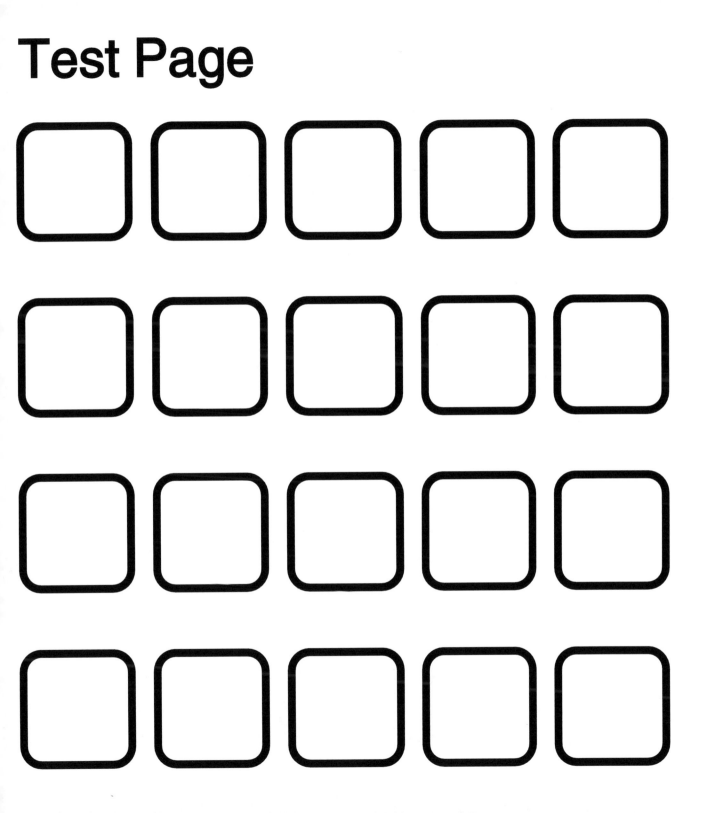

For more coloring books, visit:

RWSquaredMedia.Wordpress.com

Made in the USA
Middletown, DE
13 October 2017